THE HUNGRY GRASS

A POEM BY

A. Mary Murphy

Inanna Poetry & Fiction Series

INANNA Publications and Education Inc.
Toronto, Canada

The publisher gratefully acknowledges the support of the Canada Council for the Arts and the Ontario Arts Council for its publishing program, and the financial assistance of the Government of Canada through the Canada Book Fund.

Cover design: Val Fullard

Library and Archives Canada Cataloguing in Publication

Murphy, A. Mary (Anne Mary), 1952–, author
    The hungry grass : a poem / by A. Mary Murphy.

(Inanna poetry and fiction series)
ISBN 978-1-77133-180-7 (pbk.)

I. Title. II. Series: Inanna poetry and fiction series

PS8626.U75H85 2014   C811'.54   C2014-905732-6

MIX
Paper from
responsible sources
FSC® C004071

Printed and bound in Canada

Inanna Publications and Education Inc.
210 Founders College, York University
4700 Keele Street, Toronto, Ontario M3J 1P3 Canada
Telephone: (416) 736-5356   Fax (416) 736-5765
Email: inanna.publications@inanna.ca Website: www.inanna.ca

This is the song of my people, the music of what happened
Murphy, Brogan, Derivan, Mulcahy, Conroy
And all the ones whose names we do not know

And it is how it happened   [1833]
before fields of hungry grass
grew up over all the world
pinching us with starvation
5   herding us over the waves
that he saw me on the green
all fine in my scarlet shawl
all warm against November
all young at the parish fair
10   The ring fort on the hill top
unfarmed and unmolested
protected by daoine sidhe[1]
good people noble people
overlooks all the townland
15   looks over our house and sees
past Kelly's and Quigly's doors
from Diarmuid and Grainne's[2] bed
beyond the bustling fair green
through Fiodharta[3] village leases
20   half of them Edward Blakeney's
a few houses and gardens
a schoolhouse, teacher, and trades
past the RIC barracks
to the thousand-year churchyard
25   where St. Patrick himself stood
where St. Cíarán's[4] múinteoir[5] lived
and tutored his young pupil
where Franciscan monks were burnt

---

[1] [deena shee]: people of the mounds, the Tuatha dé Dannan, the fairies
[2] [deermud; grawnyuh]: wandering lovers, figures in Irish myth
[3] [fyurtee]: a parish in Co. Roscommon
[4] St. Ciarán of Clonmacnoise, born in Fuerty, Co. Roscommon
[5] [monchoor]: teacher

1

	martyred by Elizabeth
30	church seized under Penal Laws
	held by the Established Church
	but still a holy graveyard
	still hallowed ground for dead ones
	at the turning of the road
35	and across from Kelly's forge
	the smith just forenent[6] the pound
	stray grazing cattle and sheep
	a sharp-horned Kerry black cow
	a gentle red and white moiled
40	foraging and lowing there
	Connacht ewes and Leicester rams
	and bleating soft-wooled crossbreeds
	even a trespassing goose
	penned up by the constable
45	to be ransomed with a fine
	4s[7] a pig in corn[8]
	18s[9] for a goat
	the pound beside the milestone
	71 Irish miles
50	to Dublin City from there
	then the road curves to the right
	the far edge of the village
	turns away toward An tSuca[10]
	rushing past Castlecoote House
55	occupied by the miller
	tumbling water full of trout

---

[6]over against
[7]four shillings
[8]any cereal grain
[9]eighteen shillings
[10][sook]: a river in Co. Roscommon

2

A thousand steps from our door
along through the new village
down the hill and to the green
60   right on the Roscommon road
3 parish fairs in a year
May, August, and November
in Bealtaine[11] for summer
in Lughnasa[12] for autumn
65   and in Samhain[13] for winter
muise,[14] the noise and clamour
tinkers peddle tin and nails
Maughan, O'Reilly, and Joyce
a vardo camp on the green
70   hawkers serve oatcakes and stout
with meadowsweet to flavour
Michael Mulrain ale seller
doing robust business so
farmers sell cattle and sheep
75   McLanny, Hodson, Harkan
local stockmen making deals
breeding cows selling heifers
weavers drape drugget[15] and frieze[16]
Bryan, Turner, Clarke, and Heath
80   cloth dyed in wildflower baths
a hearty crowd of people
come from the farthest townlands
Castlestrange and Ahagad

---

[11][balltinna]: Summer
[12][loonuhsa]: Autumn, harvest
[13][sowuhn]: November, Winter
[14][musha]: indeed
[15]coarse durable woolen cloth
[16]heavy woolen cloth

Clooniquin and Ballinlegg
85 buyers, sellers, and traders
old ones counting their shillings
young ones counting their chances
wearing woven harvest knots
courting badges on display
90   And me amid the hubbub
me a local girl he knew
as Laurence Brogan's sister
as Martin Brogan's daughter
a strong and healthy daughter
95 Katie the neighbour's daughter
newcomer to the parish
from the plain of the yew trees
from Mhaigh Eo[17] 5 years before
coming here to Ros Comáin[18]
100 coming to St. Coman's wood
by Lisnaville[19] new village
living in the same parish
mile-and-a-half house to house
quick walking on the bóithrín[20]
105 to him nearby Loughtuggart
on the little An Linn Bhán[21]
kingfisher crying chee-kee
shrill and bright blue-feathered bird
quiet river full of fish
110 long-necked cormorants fishing
little lake with perch and bream

---

[17][mayoh]: Co. Mayo
[18][ross-co-main]: Co. Roscommon
[19]originally Lisnavalla, now called Lissaneaville [lisnaville]
[20][boreen]: country track
[21][an linn bawn or vawn]: Linbaun River in Co. Roscommon

the far side of Castlecoote
far end of the townland road
his 8 acres and a house
115   The Samhain fair so it was
he came selling his oat crop
10s on the barrel
14 stone[22] to a barrel
6 barrels would pay the rent
120 3 barrels for tithe and cess
125 stone
1 acre saves his leasehold
spares 7 acres for him
no danger of unpaid rent
125 the small farmer prospering
wearing a fresh báinín[23] bratt
undyed linen farmer's smock
Tim Murphy tall and pointy
was ready to take a bride
130 couldn't take a wife until
he had a place to take her
so he chose a friend to speak
sent James Kilroe to my da
to act as the go-between
135 as a neighbour to us both
cutting turf by us with Da
living in Creemully west
keeping a nursery there
keeping trees and shrubs near Tim
140 near the parish boundary
toward the Donamon road

---

[22]one stone equals fourteen pounds
[23][bawneen]: unbleached cloth

5

                    Good reasons to accept him
            generous land fresh water
            basket and thatch reeds plenty
145   bramble and heather to weave
            no other Murphy farming
            none in Castlecoote townland
            nor any in Creemully
            neither in Fiodharta parish
150   no brothers divide his land
            with Ambrose the Ribbonman
            troublemaking for land rights
            condemned and now transported
            exiled to Van Dieman's Land
155   a convict because he dared
            speak against the English king
            muise, only the landlord
            a local class of a king
            speaking speaking speaking so
160   turbulent and rebellious
            among defiant spirits
            Molly Maguires and Whiteboys
            outrageous midnight doings
            for grazier land feeds no one
165   breaking pasture for tillage
            crippling the master's livestock
            cutting the fetlock tendons
            punishing landlord's agents
            threatening all resistance
170   oath-bound solidarity
            the secret and hidden proofs
            like the articles of faith
            society membership

	men caught holding articles	
175	were as good as on the ship	
	exile if they were lucky	
	on the rope if they were not	
	courtesy King George the IV	
	transported 6 years ago	
180	before we came to Fiodharta	
	a brother I never met	

175 men caught holding articles
were as good as on the ship
exile if they were lucky
on the rope if they were not
courtesy King George the IV
transported 6 years ago
180 before we came to Fiodharta
a brother I never met
        No shame in the connection
his brother a badge of pride
I made my choice like Deirdre[24]
185 I chose my man like Niamh[25]
I loved the man like Gráinne[26]
Da agreed to make the match
2 piglets for my dowry
1 weaned from this year's farrow
190 1 to come in 2 years' time
plus share in this year's slaughter
a wealth of meat my fortune
        We walked out together so   [1834]
walked his land and saw the priest
195 Feabhra[27] 1834
we turned the sod at Imbolc[28]
firing the top to ashes
ploughing the ashes under
prayed to the Daghda's[29] daughter
200 holy Brigid of plenty

---

[24][derdruh]: defiant lover of Naoise; fated to sorrow; a figure in Irish myth
[25][neeuv]: daughter of Manannan Mac Lír, god of the sea; a figure in Irish myth
[26][grawnyuh]: wandering lover, with Diarmuid; a figure in Irish myth
[27][favra]: February
[28][imbolk]: Spring
[29][dagda]: a figure in Irish myth, whose cauldron is one of the four treasures

set out a gift of welcome
fresh butter and green rushes
the world is ready for spring
the marriage proverb says when
205   February birds do mate
then may wed nor dread to fate
the cuckoo calling wuck-oo
corncrakes cry in the meadows
        Marry before Lent or wait
210   a Feabhra bride bound for luck
no wedding from Ash Wednesday
'til after Easter Sunday
no priest would marry in Lent
no cause to wait a season
215   sure there'd been a hungry time
those days they came regular
time and then time there's wanting
and when there is please our God
next season will be better
220   sure after 4 years of want
4 hungry years in a row
next season will be better
we have enough fields to live
from this out we'll have blessings
225   that is how we prayed and hoped
gods between us and all harm
the signs were good for wedding
        My own house me just 20
a bean an tí[30] at 20
230   me the woman of the house
3 rooms, small windows, a roof

---

[30][banatee]: woman of the house

the brother's left-behind wife
the brother's fatherless son
snug in a little cottage
235   on their own small plot beside
near Tim for his protection
near me as a companion
there in my house at 20
away from my own mother
240   with no sight or sound of her
until the first month is past
equal to my own mother
equal to Celia Murphy
equal to any woman
245   we are better off than most
               Bog-oak rafters packed with scraws[31]
secure under heather thatch
stone and clay mortar footings
2-foot trenches underground
250   stone walls against the weather
with woven wattle and daub
make the walls for our 3 rooms
the gates for the craythur[32] stall
wide-mouthed hearth in the middle
255   sturdy cottage warm and dry
with nooks for nesting swallows
martins to snap up mayflies
and space for pig and childer
a cow for butter and milk
260   poultry for feathers and eggs
Timothy Murphy and me

---

[31]square sods
[32]creature

9

he offered me gold butter
beside the little river
orange-billed swans nibbling plants
265 and it is what he said there
please, Oh woman, loved by me
please give me heart, body, soul
he asked me by fresh water
    We had our mí na meala[33]
270 newly wed month of honey
to keep the fairies outside
always to bed together
a mat of new woven straw
young clover sweetens the breath
275 a thoroughly welcomed wife
is no temptation to swap
no changeling bride in this house
Peter the smith has lived here
this is a protected place
280 iron shoe above the door
clean water always inside
whitethorn grows by the threshold
dunnock hopping branch to branch
this house is sound and lucky
285 me lucky to be its wife
    20 years old and a wife
in time to sow the oat field
the feast day of St. Patrick
may the seamair óg[34] bring us luck
290 200 weight[35] of oat seed

---

[33][mee na meela]: month of honey
[34][shamrogue]: shamrock
[35]pounds

handfuls strewn over the land
a portion to the sparrow
chirruping trilling finches
the acre made for paying
295 the Landlord receives his rent
the Protestant gets his tithe
the County has its taxes
with a barrel left for seed
      Then the tenant gets to eat
300 feed his childer when they come
portion for the little cow
the pig and the laying hens
an acre of oats ourselves
can buy wool cloth or hearth crane
305 can keep until the July
can feed 2 or 3 mouths sure
an acre is 10 months' food
stone ground to meal in a quern
keep oat crumbs in our pockets
310 to keep hunger pangs away
offer oat crumbs to the sidhe[36]
the gesture of a neighbour
to have goodwill beside them
      Planting is all done in March
315 hand-cast oats and harrowing
ploughing gutters with a laigh[37]
sod and soil heaped in ridges
3 foot wide between ditches
thrush and redshank pulling worms
320 the dung heap and the ash pile

---

[36][shee]: people of the mounds, the Tuatha dé Dannan, the fairies
[37][loy]: a hand plough with a foot rest and a curved blade

75 pound bushels
hauled to the beds in keshes
hauled in keshes on our backs
straps secure across foreheads
325   strips of linen brace the load
against the strength of our necks
back and forth and back and forth
heavier than oats by half
dung and ashes and top soil
330   strewn and mixed for the praties[38]
top dressing spread with a graip[39]
          Drill the holes with a stibhín[40]
and set the sprouted cuttings
potato pieces with eyes
335   2000 pounds an acre
hoarded portion from last year
saved from our bellies for this
gogaire[41] chore to place them
bend and fold myself over
340   guggering along the rows
and Tim behind me trenching
fresh cut sod between the beds
folds over like a blanket
leaving thin canals to drain
345   uncovers insects for wrens
spares mud for shrouding murrains
soil to use for earthing up
the little 3-week plantlings
earthing again in 4 weeks

---

[38]potatoes
[39][grape]: a shovel
[40][steeveen]: a tool to make holes for potatoes
[41][guggereh]: crouched, squatting

350	more worms for watchful blackbirds
	sevenfold yield per acre
	8 tons we can trade or sell
	8 tons to store in the pit
	kept dry with ashes and cool
355	1 acre more than enough
	14 pounds a day for him
	10 or 11 feeds me
	in the heavy working times
	the weeks to break the ground up
360	move the muck and dig it in
	3 first-quality acres
	the best acres of our lease
	grow the food we eat and sell
	2 days to spread the oat seed
365	2 days to set the Lumpers
	making a small garden plot
	a patch of neeps[42] and cabbage
	2 months' field work finished so
	then move on to win the turf
370	dense black peaty plant root turf
	Cutter, holder, and spreader
	3-man team in a rhythm
	Michael Murray, John Maguire
	and Tim over in the bog
375	start the job by clearing growth
	make space on the spreading ground
	dust the surface with ashes
	to draw the water away
	pare the fum down half a foot
380	set that top layer aside

---

[42]turnips

makes poor burning in a hearth
but poor is better than none
poor burning warms the landless
sparógs[43] will cook the praties
385 potato people gather
bog cotton for cloth and beds
haul fum since they have no bog
the boys leave it by for them
then set about the cutting
390 open the bank with the blade
swift slice and toss with the sléan[44]
1 swing cutter to holder
like a bird leaps into flight
not to break the soggy brick
395 20 pounds weight a tusker
smooth pass holder to spreader
a year's turf in 7 days
whirring call of the warbler
and the pipit's vist vist vist
400 swooping birds grab up insects
disturbed and forced from cover
turf lies on the ash ground flat
pray for fresh winds in April
let the winds dry it a week
405   Then comes the time to foot it
leaning 4 curved turves on end
4 more 4 more and 4 more
more wind more drying draining
summer curing months to set
410 well-won turf ripens and burns

---

[43][spa-rohgs]: poor quality turf
[44][shlawn]: turf-cutting tool

14

a great hot fire of grógíns[45]
to keep warm and dry and fed
the fire born every morning
stirred back to life from the ash
415   Potatoes baked in ashes
potatoes boiled in their skins
potatoes fried in butter
earthing up the sprouting plants
the year's eating in the ground
420 the year's heating cut to dry
a season's work behind us
a quarter of the cycle
Bealtaine start of summer
Bealtaine coming of fire
425 May Eve close the house up snug
spread primrose on the threshold
no fairy brides or husbands
will be stolen after dark
       May morning walk the cow's field
430 combing through grasses for signs
the watchful kestrel hunting
looking for shape-shifting hares
the disguise of the old one
the hag out gathering dew
435 charming away the butter
whispering come all to me
chase her out of the pasture
break her power on the cream
garland cows with Mary gold
440 tie some primrose to their tails
protect them from evil things

---

[45][grogeens]: kindling sticks

rub the udder with blossoms
keep them fertile and milking
May Day landlords' rents are paid
445   place the sale of last year's oats
£3 in the agent's hand
paid on to Baronet Coote
living far somewhere away
leaves us plenty to go on
450   Michael Keerucan, weaver
sells frieze 1s the yard
at the May fair on the green
heavy sturdy plainweave cloth
makes wearing for a lifetime
455   all my making and patching
unbleached linen skirts and smocks
and canvas breeches for Tim
thick leggings for the wet work
for work in cheerless weather
460   and a báinín cloak for me
Tim earthing the second time
keeping spuds away from light
keeping spuds from going green
turning to deadly poison
465   more soil makes more potatoes
        Milking the bó[46] is house work
marsh marigold udder balm
protects the milk from evil
she's at the top of her milk
470   flavour the cream with ramsons
cream to churn for our butter
buttermilk for the praties

---

[46][b-oh]: cow

eating the last from the pit
the bitter 6 weeks coming
475   the firstborn báibín[47] coming
I am watching all the signs
        Thady[48] cutting meadow grass
to dry for the winter time
June grasses are in flower
480   skylarks gobble up the seeds
hay cut now grows aftergrass
the cow feeds well on eddish[49]
townland farmers shearing sheep
spinners washing and carding
485   some bales plain and some bales dyed
with madder or rud for reds
a bog water soak for black
boiled with woad for Ciarán's blue
4 spinners to a weaver
490   Celia Murphy spins all day
uses nettle juice for green
crushes iris root for black
steeps heather buds for yellow
        Work goes on in the lean months
495   May to July the meal months
fattening the barrow pig
grazing and milking the cow
picking cress by the water
collecting eggs from the hen
500   hunting like tufted herons
catching a frog here and there

---

[47][babeen]: baby
[48][tay-dy]: a familiar form for Timothy
[49][ed-ish]: second-growth grass

17

bedding the stock with flag leaves
making a haggard of whins
to keep hay up off the ground
505 wait the hundred days and more
to dig the perfect earlies
the blossoms fully open
digging only as we eat
the growing is not over
510 but the hungry weeks are passed

And the oats are ripe to cut
Lughnasa golden harvest
the August 4th parish fair
6d[50] a pound of butter
515 buys 4 pounds of ironwork
a sickle, sléan, or laigh blade
a hearth crane[51] or a pot hake[52]
2 tons of hay brings £4
corn and fruits ready to reap
520 up like thrush to the bushes
pick bilberries on the hills
purple and seedy and tart
pluck like magpies and ravens
oats all yellow for the rent
525 ready for the sickle blade

The reaping hooks are sharpened
honed keen on the strickle stone
Tim and the boys cut the stalks
smoothe work saving all the grains
530 sheaves bound with a length of straw

---

[50]six pence
[51]a bracket that can swivel pots over or away from the fire
[52]a hook for hanging pots over the hearth

deftly twisted and tucked in
bundles stooked to dry for weeks
      When potato greens wither
the beds are crowded with spuds
535   so we dig and dig and dig
seeds produce 7 to 1
8 tons of spuds an acre
2 tons go for seed and loss
every 9th potato rots
540   leaves food enough for 9 months
for a family of 6
the longest praties will keep
all the 3 crops together
to Murray's, Maguire's, to us
545   Thady carries Celia's share
loads carried home on their backs
there's plenty packed in the pit
dry in ashes and turf-mould
the 2 of us can spare some
550   sell some trade some share some so
      Hundredweight potatoes buys
a pair of woollen stockings
5 hundredweight potatoes
gets a pair of brogues for Tim
555   from Neilan in Creemully
for the bog but only there
or in the fields in the wet
most weather we go barefoot
or sometimes wear pampooties
560   made from a little rawhide
      The carting home just half done
the oats and the turf are dry

good dry turves at 2 pound weight
carry them home in a creel
565 30 bricks to a basket
90 trips back to the bog
ricking the bricks in shelter
stacking the sods in the loft
curing it with rising smoke
570 the 3 lads work together
whatever the hauling is
then is September over
and after the turves the oats
                    The food and the heat are saved
575 and the rent needs threshing now
sheaves and sheaves brought in the house
for nowhere could be drier
secure the corn from buntings
from the sparrow and linnet
580 pecking by the door for seeds
scutching the oats in rhythm
scutch scutch scutch scutch scutch scutch scutch
scutch to spare the straw for mats
shake the oats out on the floor
585 sweep it up for winnowing
toss the grains out in the air
into the wind from the tray
the chaff is caught on the breeze
clean seed collected to sell
590   Bog, lazy beds, meadow, field
potatoes, turf, hay, and corn
do not go empty handed
wherever it is you go
8 months of constant labour

595	and every day the fire burns
	to cook the praties cook the
	praties cook the praties cook
	boil and bake and fry 3 times
	milk the cow and feed the pig
600	mash and mix the pig's portion
	churn the butter find the eggs
	and feel the báibín moving

          The meitheal[53] year is finished

hard months of work in éineacht[54]

605   all labour done together

potatoes and corn go leór[55]

and townlands will have feasting

Da and the boys kill their pig

the blood and head and trotters

610   hopeful croaking rooks and crows

demanding some guts to eat

black pudding and bacon flitch

everything use nothing waste

smoked in the hearthfire a week

615   griscín[56] and crúibín[57] are shared

chops and pig's feet good eating

my dowry share of the pig

everything that can be saved

picked gathered preserved and stored

620   Feasting far beyond fullness

mighty dinner and dancing

dancing well beyond breathless

---

[53][meh-hull]: communal labour
[54][in aynukht]: done together
[55][galore]: sufficiency
[56][griskeen]: pork loin
[57][croobeen]: pig's foot

21

drink stout porter and póitín[58]
drinking way beyond meisce[59]
625   the neighbour a drunken gawm[60]
a crúiscín[61] of drink taken
completes the harvest quarter
at Samhain start of winter
now the púca[62] is afield
630   spoiling any food unpicked
be wary all November
of dancing merry fairies
abroad on all the hillsides
leading wanderers astray
635   Tim is after cutting rods
sally rods for his hand work
willow work done in winter
weaving clíabhs[63] to carry turf
ciséan[64] to strain potatoes
640   we sit around the basket
3 times a day in summer
twice only in the winter
eating less when working less
eating only just enough
645   a store of oats to keep us
harvest has been good to us
don't return waste for plenty
        In November on the green

---

[58][potcheen]: traditional distilled drink
[59][meshkyuh]: drunk
[60]simpleton
[61][croosh-keen]: a small jar or jug
[62][pooka]: feared and mischievous fairy
[63][cleeves]: basket
[64][kihshawn]: tray-like basket for straining potatoes

the rent oats are safely sold
650 the winter birds have returned
and the winter work begun
redwings picking rowan fruit
silent grebes fishing the pond
and Tim's calloused hands take up
655 the soft straw saved from scutching
plait it into sleeping mats
straw doors and windows shut tight
shield against the wet and wind
keep the animals secure
660 straw thatch repairs the rooftop
a pair of small stools hearthside
3-legged creepies to perch
down low out of the turf smoke
          Perch after milking the cow
665 sit after mashing the feed
rest after mucking the dung
wait for the growing leanbh[65]
they say carry high a girl
they say carry low a boy
670 in 3 more months we will know
pass the evenings with stories
start the traditional way
there were good times once, not yours
not mine, but somebody's time
675 airneán[66] by the hearthside
gather and talk and tell tales
of Paudyeen and the weasel
and the man who drank a lake

---

[65] [lannuv]: child
[66] [arneh-an]: gathering for talk

	meeting in neighbours' houses
680	back and forth the winter time
	2 ways to tell a story
	and 12 ways to sing a song
	after the darkest days pass
	after the holly is hung
685	after the candle is burnt
	to welcome the Christ child's birth
	we'll be ready for Imbolc
	after Imbolc we will know [1835]
	guard the door with Brigid's cross
690	fresh woven with new rushes
	invite her O tar isteach[67]
	and welcome her to the house
	lay cloth across the threshold
	for Brid to bless in passing
695	a cloak to use in childbirth
	invoking her protection
	and after St. Brigid's feast
	after song birds trill the spring
	after the wedding season
700	the time is ready for me
	wearing my Thady's waistcoat
	for him to share the birth pain
	he eases the way for me
	burdened with a heavy stone
705	he circles the house for me
	carries half my suffering
	Celia's hand to attend me
	Brigid's cloth across my brow
	shields me from waiting evil

---

[67][tahr ish-tyahk]: come in

24

710   1 year married and a babe
        1 cycle after we wed
        Bridget after my mother
        St. Bride, Mary of the Gael
        a girl to celebrate spring
715   February 24th
        come to the small farmer's house
        never had I lived a year
        never that pleased me better
        hurry oatmeal in my mouth
720   hurry butter in bábóg's[68]
        a piece of Peter's iron
        tucked into her little dress
        everyone say God bless it
        every caution taken so
725   every last protection done
        immersed 3 times in water
        the fairies cannot take her
        then I drink the herbal root
        bitter-tasting milkwort tea
730   lus an bhainne[69] brings sweet milk
        the baby will not hunger
        the watching women keep us
        guard us until the churching
        the baby's name a secret
735   spoken out to no one 'til
        we stand in front of the priest
                21 and a mother
        in time to sow the oat field
        the feast day of St. Patrick

---

[68][babogue]: baby
[69][lus an vanyuh]: milkwort, a bluebell

740   may the seamair óg bring us luck
          wear a sprig of young clover
          then drown the green leaf in drink
          draining the Pota Pádraig[70]
          drinking health and toast the saint
745   sweeping with a besom broom
          spreading woodruff on the floors
          strewing myrtle on the bed
          freshen air and banish fleas
          gather cipíns[71] for kindling
750   coaxing the fire back alive
          another year of spuds in
          another year of oats cast
          another year of turf cut
          another year of rent paid
755   field and beds and bog all worked
          the little garden seeded
          the hat tipped to the landlord
                 May fair trading all well done
          in a din of faction fights
760   hum of Traveller Shelta
          Luke Makelly the butcher
          makes offer for this year's calf
          when the weaning time is come
          handshake done Tim moves along
765   and bargains a load of turf
          the stud price we will pay to
          take the cow over the field
          to be bred by James Burne's bull
          sell what we don't need ourselves

---

[70][porig]: Patrick
[71][chipeens]: kindling sticks

770	buy what we can't make ourselves
	trade what we won't miss ourselves
	cloth for Bridget's little clothes
	for a drugget skirt for me
	needles from the tinker man
775	and thread they make from nettles
	sewing is quieter work
	Now come the summer lean weeks
	brachán neantóg[72] sustains us
	oatmeal and nettle porridge
780	nettles to increase my milk
	keep the bábóg thriving so
	and nettles to cleanse our blood
	meal to stave off the hunger
	give strength to work the lean time
785	letting a little cow's blood
	black pudding of blood and meal
	drisín[73] flavoured with tansy
	sausage of sheep's blood and milk
	then the earlies are ready
790	and berry season ripens
	blackberry and raspberry
	growing wild and plentiful
	sweet and juicy in the hills
	anxious pigeons and robins
795	flapping around the bushes
	eating every fruit they can
	eating while they can get it
	Lughnasa marks the turning
	the harvest cycle begins

---

[72][brawkan nyantoke]: porridge of nettles and oatmeal
[73][drisheen]: a sort of black pudding, made from cow or sheep blood

800	gathering all the wild food
	selling some eggs now and then
	cutting the golden oat stalks
	hauling the year's spade of turf
	digging the tons of praties
805	killing the first dowry pig
	smoking a flitch of bacon
	making ready for winter
	snipe and plover in the bog
	after Samhain eve the frost
810	the bó goes dry for 2 months
	the berries and charlock done
	praties and a bowl of meal
	ground as we need in the quern
	the only food until spring
815	taken with rounds of stories
	of the greedy alt-luachra[74]
	of Crinnawn and his power
	of Fionn[75] and his great hound Bran
	Baby suffered with a cough
820	barking like a fox at night
	powdered honeysuckle leaves
	protect her from the fever
	ragwort to soothe the hacking
	tea of druid meadowsweet
825	keeping her from the death kiss
	she a cushla geal mo chroidhe[76]
	the beating voice of my heart
	gods between us and all harm

---

[74][lew-kra]: an evil, greedy fairy
[75][Finn]: Fionn Mac Chumhaill [Mac Cool] of the Fianna
[76][a cooshla gyall ma cree]: the vein, the pulse, the beating voice of my heart

dried flowers and roots and leaves
830 preserved so they preserve us
tonics and cures for complaints
the child is not a year yet   [1836]
but fierce as heather she is
eyes blue as Conall Cearnach's[77]
835 cheeks foxglove red like Deirdre
please god not a stolen child
we fear the jealous fairies
protect her from all evil
fine hot fire against the cold
840 plant remedies for their cures
prayers and rites deliver her
and the solstice brings the light
the year is turning for spring
2 months eating spuds and oats
845 3 months dreaming of cresses
greening sign of Lady Day
just 1 month until the calf
ah sure God be with the days
    A fine little heifer calf
850 a little dun cow to sell
milk again after 2 months
buttermilk for the oat meal
field work begins at Imbolc
manure and ashes and earth
855 digging and labouring months
Celia tends to our Bridget
the bábóg plays in hearth warmth
drifts asleep in afternoons
lulled by the clack of the wheel

---

[77][cayr-nach]: chief warrior of the Red Branch, a figure in Irish myth

860   click and whir Celia spinning
          so I can bear my work share
          creel after creel on my back
          her boy comes with us along
          9 years old and hearty so
865   he digs like a little man
          and we live our clachan[78] life
                 News reaches out from Dublin
          passed from mouth to mouth to mouth
          O'Connell is there beyond
870   in London making speeches
          England never will be just
          never willingly at all
          the Irish Liberator
          a tireless class of a man
875   insists and warns the tyrants
          Ireland will not cease to seek
          if it takes a hundred years
          while tyrants ask what to do
          about the destitute poor
880   that are everywhere around
          the Catholic peasant poor
          but they care nothing for us
          only for their own comfort
          local societies grow
885   the men meet in secret so
          restless for the right to land
          the memory of Ambrose
          brother Ambrose gone and lost
          never heard of since he sailed
890   gone into the west martyred

---

[78][clah-hawn]: co-operative life among a cluster of cottages

for all his trouble alone
his poor wife and child with us
no speeches and hushed meetings
change what needs done every day
895   Rent oats are cast on the field
pigeons swooping for the grains
long-tailed pheasants foraging
dragging blue-green tail feathers
peck and strut across the field
900 praties are set in the ground
covered with a shroud of soil
neeps and cabbage are planted
turf is cut with John and Mike
the Dexter heavy with milk
905 safely into Bealtaine
sun and rain on spuds and oats
leverets in the meadows
owls hoot and scan for movement
short sharp cry of the kestrel
910 swooping and snatching a mouse
otters slip in the river
teaching their pups how to swim
and the calf is weaned and sold
in August for near £5
915 hide the sparán[79] in the thatch
well into our third good year
        But this year there's poor harvest
this year crowded with people
this year hunger starts to spread
920 the parish so full of mouths
spailpín[80] and spinner wanting

---

[79][spa-rawn]: purse

just a few sound potatoes
they'll be destitute by March
they'll get their deaths this winter
925   they'll be away on the ships
migrant labour pays the rent
double rents for conacre
and now the pits are rotting
not enough to feed them all
930   8d a day for labour
to buy food that isn't there
even if gentry hired them
weavers commission no yarn
measure out what they have stored
935   sell yards of frieze and drugget
but buy no more stocks of thread
wheels and treadles click and hum
growing colourful spindles
scarlet and yellow and green
940   hoping for a miracle
to come to come God to come
we help Celia make her rent
our duty to a sister
spinners and the landless ones
945   they always suffer hardest
whenever the lean times come
no leases to sustain them
the migrant and dependent
working to earn all their food
950   poor harvest means no earning
by late September we know
another báibín coming

---

[80][spalpeen]: a migratory labourer

32

by late September we know
a hungry winter coming
955   for the landless among us
with their harvest cut in half
and nothing ever but spuds
the animals sustain us
and a portion of the oats
960   kill the second barrow pig
the last share of my dowry
share of meat to the neighbours
share from their slaughter to us
puddings made and trotters cooked
965   the carcass over the fire
cures a week over wood smoke
flitches cut and smoked again
        Hungry half-naked people
pawning their clothes to buy meal
970   living on cabbage for days
scrabble in the dirt for neeps
gaimbín[81] men sniffing around
lend shillings at gougers' rates
people in their thousands go
975   people walk away to ships
people vanish every day
poor harvest clearing the land
agents happy when they leave
many are too poor to go
980   sit in their hovels and die
cautious and careful winter
counting out the potatoes
count every day 1 by 1

---

[81][gombeen]; wheeler dealer, usurer

33

for Tim, for me, for Celia
985 for the childer hers and ours
spare an egg for a beggar
fear watches in every house
watches the cow and the pig
watches every grain of oats
990 watches and counts and measures
bodies fold themselves in so
fear is after hunting here
it is breaking my heart is
gets grief from the bitter year
995 we start to talk of going
take ship to the Kanadies[82]
go where we could own the land
go where the land won't fail us
go where the land is open
1000 we start to talk of going
the sparán marked for the fares
it is long the winter is
the hungry weaken and wait
huddle around with stories
1005 with tales of lucky meetings
a share with the good people
a share of money or land
to try will they be able
let on that there is comfort
1010 what do we do only wait
and listen to the groaning
ochone mo mhuirnín mo croidhe[83]
sorrow my darling my heart

---

[82]Upper and Lower Canada
[83][o hone ma voorneen ma cree]: oh sorrow, my darling, my heart

34

keening across the townlands
1015 we are better off than most
we have stocks and will not starve
we have enough for planting
never eat the precious seed
never risk our doom the way
1020 give a little sip of milk
give a small taste of butter
give a potato in alms
when walking bones plead for food
    St. Bridget keep us from want
1025 gods between us and all harm
deliver us from hunger
we all have turf to warm us
even the hungry are warm
the hoarders and forestallers
1030 withhold to drive up prices
on food almost none can buy
a great desire coming on
to stop there and kill themselves
them that gain from suffering
1035 stocks of oats in their haggard
pits of praties under guard
only for God we'd do it
only for fear of God so
not yet the beasts they treat us
1040 a vile slíbhín[84] class of man
not in friendship the man comes
that is seen along like that
vicious as a hunting stoat
prowling along the bóthrín

---

[84][sleeveen]: an untrustworthy person

1045　sharp teeth all ready to gut
　　　　　　And the weather turns for Spring　　[1837]
　　　prayers go up for the new crop
　　　praties go into the ground
　　　rent sits safe in the sparán
1050　other ones not so lucky
　　　pawn their tools to make the rent
　　　heavy with the second child
　　　my labour is saved for that
　　　the planting does without me
1055　the hauling on other backs
　　　Celia and her boy step to
　　　strewing the ash and the dung
　　　setting the sprouted pieces
　　　Thady in his straw cáibín[85]
1060　guggering and trenching beds
　　　curlews pull up worms to eat
　　　lapwings with their short pink legs
　　　darting about for beetles
　　　wee Bridget at 2 years old
1065　tries her hand at setting spuds
　　　seeding neeps and cabbages
　　　learning the work in the beds
　　　I milk and churn and gather
　　　butter cream eggs and cresses
1070　moil and toil from task to task
　　　　　　Aibreán[86] comes for cutting turf
　　　for laying on the brat Bhride[87]
　　　Brigid's cloak to ease my way

---

[85][cawbeen]: hat
[86][ab-rown]: April
[87][brat breed]: Brigid's cloak

a fine month to have a birth
1075 the bábóg[88] mo bhuachaill[89]
Celia my handywoman
with me again for the birth
saining[90] him to guard from harm
the 3 drops on his forehead
1080 Father, Son, and Holy Ghost
wash him with the 9 wavelets
for his voice, form, and sweet speech
for his luck, health, and goodness
for his throat, pluck, and for grace
1085 bind a burnt cloth at the cord
all the rites to protect him
and keep him safe from poc sí[91]
but still he is fairy struck
a fine month to have a birth
1090 but a harsh year to be born
with a new queen in England
August to August hunger
shadowy omens on us
pray over watch over him
1095 John's Wort in his left armpit
the fairy doctor's yarrow
honeysuckle tucked around
power against bad spirits
a sip of Tae na gCailleach[92]
1100 like our Mayo people use
try everything everything

---

[88][babogue]: baby
[89][ma voo-a-kull]: my boy
[90]protective birth rituals
[91][puck shee]: fairy struck
[92][kye-luhkh]: wise hag, Celtic goddess of Winter

37

for a wasting sickly babe
my boy our baby Peter
his father's father honoured
1105 his name for the firstborn son
naming pattern son to son
Peter the smith then Patrick
then Peter again then Tim
and now our little Peter
1110 God bless him and save his soul
my heart stinging with nettles
my heart a desolate place
my heart is breaking in halves
mother of a taken child
1115   The keening carries the news
Celia comes to lay him out
washes his little body
Thady buys dúidíns[93] and plug
must be pipes and tobacco
1120 a token of food and drink
our near neighbours come to wake
reap grief from the bitter wind
Boyds and Conboys and Morans
Wards, M'Governs, and Mannions
1125 come to watch and wake with us
our partners John and Michael
Owen comes from the village
Brogans come from Lisnaville
smell the scent of Caoilte's[94] skin
1130 on the notes of our lament
flowers cover his small corpse

---

[93][doodeens]: clay pipes
[94][kweeltuh]: a figure in Irish myth, a poet of the Fianna

marigold and primrose blooms
shield his spirit from evil
pipe smoke keeps evil away
1135 keeps it from finding his soul
decades of the Rosary
at the end of the waking
the sorrowful mysteries
agony in the garden
1140 the scourging at the pillar
the coronation with thorns
the carrying of the cross
and last the crucifixion
it is broken my heart is
1145 like the Mother's at the cross
with bearing the will of God
Thady bears the little box
along to Fiodharta churchyard
in the clay on the south side
1150 to lie with his Murphy kin
gods between us and all harm
          A bitter kind of reaping
in the midst of Lughnasa
what to do only bear it
1155 carry away the baby
and carry home the praties
carry home the turf and oats
carry our sorrow with us
brambles picked from the hillsides
1160 a mighty harvest feasting
and October ends in frost
buy a pig from the sparán
the crop of oats and praties

carefully scutched and pitted
1165   a better winter than last
the way we will not hunger
from this out we will not starve
ah sure, God be with the days
                Samhain and the winter birds
1170   black-headed gull and fieldfare
harsh birdcall tells the season
leave the raspberries hanging
once the púca is abroad
the month of fairy revels
1175   badgers and hares in burrows
the people safe in houses
don't dare to go out at night
the woven-straw door pulled close
until the light of the day
1180   frees us to outside labour
mucking the stall piling dung
cut and carry sally rods
for Thady's winter weaving
feed the cow and feed the hens
1185   no milk from the cow these months
no butter to churn for sale
save eggs for feeding Bridget
sell the oats and make the rent
make a few extra shillings
1190   buy cloth and thread and needles
good harvest means good market
hunker down on the creepies[95]
sit low by the glowing fire
Thady weaving the pardógs[96]

---

[95]three-legged stools

1195   to carry turf from the bog
       twists straw for a sugán[97] chair
       I patching tears in his bratt
       sewing Bridget's little dress
       telling stories and riddles
1200   white as flour but isn't flour
       green as grass but isn't grass
       red as blood but isn't blood
       black as ink but isn't ink
       the blackberry bloom to fruit
1205   piecework and tales pass winter
       and Bridget is coming 3

              Happy with a barrow pig   [1838]
       fattening here in the house
       able for it every year
1210   knowing how could we buy it
       knowing how could we feed it
       knowing how are we lucky
       could give it a share of spuds
       have a luxury of meat
1215   to feed us or pay the rent
       if trouble comes on the land
       soon the bó will calve again
       there will be milk and butter
       the days are like a feasting
1220   around the Daghda's cauldron
       and Brigid's morning rises
       bringing Imbolc and the light
       turning the sod our fifth time
       the yellow breasted wagtails

---

[96][par-dohgs]: large baskets
[97][shoo-gawn]: twisted straw

41

1225   scrabble the soil for insects
        with every lift of the laigh
        every house in the parish
        praying God be with the days
        carry creels of ash and dung
1230   dig it down into the clay
        beds are made ready for seed
        rabbits out of their burrows
        at first growth of the grasses
        a new woven Brigid's cross
1235   hung in the house protects us
        fresh rushes strewn on the floor
        lift the house out of winter
        pink bellied tits with long tails
        and yellow breasted blue tits
1240   snatching every seed they can
        gorging as Thady spreads oats
        the feast day of St. Pádraig
        the sléan is sharp for Aibreán
        the spreading ground made ready
1245   ashes to draw the water
        the bog is full of cutters
        every man in the parish
        cutting his year's worth of bricks
        letting it rest a few weeks
1250   draining its weight of water
        marsh marigold and primrose
        garland the cow to shield her
        protect her and save her milk
        chase the hag from the meadow
1255   Bealtaine and the first fair
        Makelly buys the new calf

a few pounds in the sparán
kept hidden there in the thatch
against the next time of need
1260 against the hope of passage
thank God tithe is abolished
payment to the Protestant
collected like the taxes
from an unwilling people
1265 faithful Catholic people
forced to pay the unjust rate
until the tithe wars broke it
feel the peace of abundance
a share with the good people
1270 quiet call of the warblers
along the edge of the bog
feeding on tiny craythurs
as the boys are footing turf
the soft fresh breezes blowing
1275 all around the drying bricks
              Earthing up and clearing weeds
mucking out the cow and pig
picking nettles for porridge
eating the cresses like Fionn
1280 bleeding the cow a little
measuring out the praties
waiting for the wee earlies
waiting to see the July
sighing thanks across townlands
1285 freshening like the breezes
ending the months of worry
starting the months of reaping
meadow grass for the haggard

hay is worth £2 a ton
1290   dry and ready for stacking
        yellow oats ready to cut
        bilberries ready to pick
        turf well won and in the loft
        praties dug and in the pit
1295   the barrow slaughtered and smoked
        food and fuel and rent all saved
        feasting, drinking, and dancing
        mark the end of Lughnasa
        mark the long year of our grief
1300   since our Peter died from us
        another báibín coming
        gods between us and all harm
                    Samhain eve we close the door
        put our hands to winter work
1305   the sharpening and patching
        wash Peter's little dresses
        reeking with turf smoke they are
        hang them out on the thorn bush
        ready for the growing one
1310   arneán with the Murrays
        with Maguires and Celia by
        hear Deirdre of the Sorrows
        the tale with the sea pirate
        tell The Hags of the Long Teeth
1315   the big black dog to guard them
        and the priest the dog struck mute
        muise, but I love that one
        take 1 tale and pay with 2
        the way we pass the winter
1320   daylight tending the craythurs

we muck and feed and gather
evenings in talk and stories
beside the glowing turf fire
holly around the windows
1325   shining green around the door
shelters the woodland fairies
through the cold of solstice night
catches at evil spirits
seeking to enter the house
1330   it was pleasant were the days
passing a peaceful winter
         Until St. Cera's[98] death day   [1839]
a night for fairy revels
Eanáir[99] 1839
1335   buried in a heavy snow
a happy snowy morning
a Little Christmas morning
a Nollaig na mBan[100] morning
became the end of the world
1340   melting to a sticky heat
a queer hushed pause, a stillness
thick heavy cloud descended
a day swathed in bog cotton
this now is the story so
1345   no bird in song on the wing
not a wisp of air moving
not even holly trembling
craythurs took to their coverts
spoken word floating a mile

---

[98][kare-a or kee-ra]: an Irish abbess
[99][an-awr]: January
[100][null-ag na man]: Women's Christmas

1350   like a great holding of breath
then the sky began to blow
whispered stirring from the west
it came all in a sudden
Oíche na Gaoíthe Móire[101]

1355   a freshening quickening
expanding shuddering push
the gates of heaven closing
with a force after twelfth night
a cruel class of a wind

1360   bean sí[102] howling muscled wind
cold again and pelting hail
rafters groaning and cracking
fish and salt water raining
this many miles from the sea

1365   roofs lifting off and flying
crows thundering to the ground
hearths erupting like bonfires
wind like a giant's bellows
sparks swarm like clouds of fireflies

1370   if the wind breaks in the door
wind throwing down the houses
like an eviction crowbar
pyre to pyre like druid fires
sheep swept into the river

1375   cattle drowning in the bog
trees ripping out of the earth
yanked by the roots like cipíns
like kindling sticks and matches
God between us and all harm

---

[101][eekhya na gweeha moyra]: The Night of the Big Wind
[102][banshee]: a fairy woman, death messenger

46

1380 in our fright didn't we pray
prayers begging storming heaven
the heavens besieging us
Our Father and Hail Mary
the Glory Be and the Creed
1385 all the Sunday Mysteries
5 Glorious Mysteries
and 5 Joyful Mysteries
Glory be to the Father
Mary pray for us sinners
1390 first the annunciation
the visitation the birth
resurrection ascension
assumption coronation
I desire and I desire
1395 the grace of a holy death
repeated and repeated
Rosary on Rosary
ceaseless motion of the beads
on our knees all through the night
1400 clutching Bridget between us
fearing the day of judgement
until the great wind is spent
breathlessly yields to the day
        In the morning we are saved
1405 smell of salt smell of seaweed
the land littered with dead birds
stocks of oats from the haggard
strewn around like fresh rushes
grasses swept back to meadows
1410 feed now for fairy horses
men plunged down in cold water

women thrown into the trees
childer hidden in baskets
no one spared from the frenzy
1415 little cabins swept away
roofs altogether blown off
swept with a mighty fury
we take stock in the morning
half our roof thatch ripped away
1420 turf blown and thrown from the loft
the precious sparán with it
the carefully counted pounds
the extra shillings and pence
for the rent and for the cess
1425 for the little extra things
for fares to the Kanadies
disaster for us it is
God between us and all harm
oh that we didn't linger
1430 to see what this day has brought
to start all over again
how to pay for anything
how not be put on the road
we are luckier than most
1435 we are all of us alive
the cow and pig delivered
always kept nights in the stall
bellowed and squealed all the night
our sturdy house is standing
1440 the spuds are safe in the pits
Bridget held safe between us
the bábóg stays safe within
the townland is a ruin

         the parish and the county
1445   the world is blown to pieces
         we piece it back together
         give thanks to God who spared us
         neighbours working together
         rushing when the shock is past
1450   salvaging what can be saved
         hasty cutting and curing
         plenty of wood for the fires
         cipíns and grógins go leór
         let no storm-killed meat be waste
1455   meitheal labour every hour
         every skill and trade and arm
         to rebuild what was broken
         to gather what was scattered
         to revive what was our hope
1460   outdoor work out of season
         in the biting winter wet
         thatching waits for reeds and straw
         everywhere people praying
         a hum of Lord have mercy
1465   Lord help us Mary help us
         5 years filling the sparán
         blown to far parts of the world
         how make the rent in 4 months
         how feed the cow without hay
1470   the pig bought in November
         needs sold at market in May
         can't be kept for October
         can't be fattened for our meat
         the cow will calve in a month
1475   the calf is for market too

offer Makelly the both
feed them all on potatoes
ration the praties and oats
count out what to hoard for seed
1480   break ground again at Imbolc
and the struggle starts again
hand to mouth and field to house
day by day by day by day
seed in the ground and turf cut
1485   valuers in the parish
counting measuring writing
filling pages of notebooks
house books field books tenant books
valuing for rent and tax
1490   lucky half the roof is gone
be grateful for small mercies
improvements of years laid waste
means no increase to the rent
        Bealtaine weather a sign
1495   that harvest will bring plenty
Bealtaine rough and rainy
say the old ones all around
sure a wet and windy May
fills the yard with corn and hay
1500   then on a late May morning
breith clainne[103] comes upon me
I put on Thady's frieze bheist[104]
call Celia here to help me
lay Brigid's cloth over me
1505   bring mo bhuachaill from me

---

[103][b-zhay klonyuh]: childbirth
[104][beest]: waistcoat

sain the baby when he comes
a hearty new son for us
a son with big hands for us
3 drops onto his forehead
1510 9 wavelets onto his flesh
3 spittles onto his cheek
put butter into his mouth
put iron into his dress
fairies will try to take him
1515 covet a strong human boy
every eye to look at him
must say aloud God bless it
God between us and all harm
we've no shilling for the priest
1520 since the night of the big wind
3 droplets from Thady's hand
Father, Son, and Holy Ghost
name him John for the smith's son
brother of Thady's grandda
1525 we dare not name him Peter
not for generations yet
bring the luck back to bless us
          Peace now after our trouble
the lucky bábóg turns things
1530 hunger and tempest are gone
muise, God be with the days
what do we do only live
hear the shrill call of the swift
nesting in the open roof
1535 swooping dark after midges
only Bealtaine birds now
only the migrants are here

no sound of resident birds
the ones here every season
1540 their mellow calls gone silent
carried away on the wind
blackcap and treecreeper gone
strange to see no robin here
since the Little Christmas wind
1545 since the Ballinagare[105] wind
blown who knows where are they gone
when the winds will bring them back
windfall trees become rafters
summer grasses become thatch
1550 Bealtaine labour doubled
mending our broken houses
replacing broken haggards
racing the sun to Samhain
close the roof before the cold
1555 still footing and earthing up
still cutting oats and mucking
still picking eggs and berries
it is good enough it is
      And the next year is the same   [1840]
1560 O'Connell and O'Brien
Union repeal, Young Ireland
Catholic and Protestant
the pacifists and rebels
want to rule ourselves alone
1565 sure now God be with the days
we're long after trying so
educated class of men
strive like Ambrose did that time

---

[105][bal-in-a-gar]: a village in north-west Co. Roscommon

	want the fields we dig our own
1570	we dig while we are waiting
	and another year has done
	and we are 7 years wed
	Bridget a stór[106] is 6 years
	John mo bhuachaill is 2
1575	another báibín coming
	grows like rushes in Imbolc
	grows like dock in Bealtaine
	grows like corn in Lughnasa
	ready to come in Samhain
1580	named for the mother's father
	the eve of St. Martin's feast
	we have carried home the turf
	reaped the oats dug the praties
	gathered the hay picked berries
1585	and brought Martin to the house
	a thriving son to the house
	sweet-natured son to the house
	the cold and snow stay outdoors
	the hearthfire never goes out
1590	animal heat from the stall
	Thady bending wattle gates
	plaiting marram grass for rope
	keep the cow from wandering
	I mending and sewing clothes
1595	brewing honeysuckle leaves
	against the childers' fever
	mallow poultice for the rash
	iris root against toothache
	it was a safe time that time

[1841]

106[asthore]: treasure

53

1600   but if it was we knew so
        a sweet dream of violets
        it meant riches came to us

              Breaking the ground at Imbolc   [1842]

        Thady is after digging
1605   turning in the ash and dung
        Celia's boy is 15 years
        works his acre like a man
        working by John and Michael
        fields ready for spuds and oats
1610   I tend the bó and her calf
        cook potatoes 'til they're gone
        bit of meal with buttermilk
        gather sorrel and cresses
        able to feed the childer
1615   spread bog myrtle against fleas
        drying meadowsweet for cures
        foxglove for burns and swellings
        Bridget a help with the boys
        carries and changes Martin
1620   keeps John from straying away
        falling into the river
        pulled under by the bean fionn[107]
        muise, it's a meitheal life
        even the pine martens help
1625   keep rats and mice from the oats
        and after the rent is made
        there's extra in the sparán
        maybe in another year
        maybe we will have a shoat
1630   we are luckier than most

---

[107][ban finn]: a water fairy who will reach up and pull children under

arneán with the neighbours
Thady playing the whistle
Michael and John telling tales
The Tailor and the Three Beasts
1635 and The King of Ireland's Son
all singing The Croppy Boy
all singing Handsome Sally
passing the dark of the year
passing St. Martin's feast day
1640 passing St. Brigid's feast day   [1843]
shake green rushes in welcome
an offering of butter
fire the top and turn the sod
dig plant cut dry reap haul thresh
1645 the daily work of 9 months
ends with a little girleen
called Ann for Thady's mother
Samhain baby like Martin
into a house of stories
1650 riddles and whistles and songs
warm and dry and fed a stór
        Vervain against evil eye   [1844]
among the most sacred herbs
keeps away jealous fairies
1655 it is pleasant are the years
gods between us and all harm
10 years now we are married
the parish is emptying
well over a thousand souls
1660 are dead or emigrated
scattered far in those 10 years
no future for any here

we work and fill the sparán
5 childer, 4 are living
1665 hard times come but we get on
ochone[108] we have a sorrow
since our Peter died from us
God bless him and save his soul
it is getting on we are
1670 5 years beyond the tempest
it is long our journey is
but if it is we prosper
this year a pig in the house
the bó will soon drop her calf
1675 the rent safe in the sparán
every shilling we can spare
saving again for our fares
Bridget my help is 9 years
John near 5, Martin just 3
1680 and Ann a leanbh 3 months
when we break sod at Imbolc
and at the end of summer
Garland Sunday[109] we give thanks
climbing the bilberry hills
1685 tenfold thanks at Lughnasa
          All the townlands pass the news
it is soon told how it is
the Healy sisters are hanged
hanged outside Roscommon jail
1690 who murdered Patrick Bryan
Kate Healy's husband that was
Bridget Lanigan's in-law

---

[108][och-ohn]: a sorrow from the past that is still present
[109]the last Sunday of July

what way are they the sisters
murdering class of women
1695 they would do revenge on him
God preserve their mortal souls
what is it a husband does
for a wife to want revenge
for a sister to help her
1700 Thady my husband mo croidhe[110]
no Catherine Bryan me
he shelters me like Diarmuid
covers the bed with rushes
has a heart for our childer
1705 never spares his back from work
it is a fine man he is
I am lucky in the match
hard times remind us we sin
good times remind God loves us
1710 the harvest and hauling done
another crop in the pit
less of it to trade or sell
more of it for the belly
as the childer get older
1715 get older and more of them
By Brigid's Day it is sure   [1845]
another bábóg will come
ag iompar clainne[111] I am
our sturdy house is filling
1720 a 7th mouth to join us
sleep in the family bed
in Lughnasa it will come

---

[110][ma-cree]: my heart
[111][aig umper klonyuh]: pregnant

57

with all the other reaping
now the steady round of days
1725 moves out to the fields and bogs
dig and haul and use our feet
laigh and creel a part of us
like our arms and backs they are
when last year's praties are done
1730 picking greens by the river
delicate spindly cresses
big bunches of green sorrel
tall yellow-blossomed charlock
cool the butter in the bog
1735 grind oats in the little quern
boil meal in a little milk
eat well until the July
then the earlies are ready
dig every day for that day
1740 the crop looks grand so it does
give thanks on Garland Sunday
Fraochán[112] Sunday on the hills
picking plump ripe bilberries
eating our fill drying more
1745 mash some for violet dye
a soak for Celia's frieze threads
oats and hay are ripe and cut
the praties ready to dig
untimely rain is falling
1750 rain running in the trenches
and then spots come on some leaves
blackish spots with a white ring
some plants do start to wither

---

[112][frocken]: another name for bilberries

Thady pulls the rotting stalks
1755 digs under the blackened leaves
rot above means rot below
cutting the plants won't stop it
get them dug and in the pits
there's a panic of digging
1760 breith clainne comes upon me
God between us and all harm
it is the last thing I need
the last another báibín
Celia here along to help
1765 here to help me every time
sain the baby when she comes
third daughters named for mothers
named Catherine after me
a third share of the crop lost
1770 maybe as much as a half
some of the pits are rotted
still it is food enough here
oats flax bere barley and wheat
but if it is it is sold
1775 it is loaded onto ships
is sailed across to England
with the meat sold on fair days
as though from a foreign farm
belonging to the English
1780 secret societies roused
threaten landlords and agents
the landless people suffer
we are luckier than most
we have half a crop in stores
1785 we hear talk of ravages

cruel wet harvest weather
in parishes farther west
not enough in the sparán
to take all of us away
1790   muise, God be with the days
                Too late to be going now
ships set out after Imbolc
when weather is not so harsh
there's money enough for 1
1795   hard times keep coming on us
at the mercy of our fate
labour on land that's not ours
here at the landlord's fancy
perish doing work all year
1800   always in fear of the road
begin to talk together
begin to talk of going
and it is what we give out
Thady must leave us behind
1805   what will he do only go
he will stay to plant the crop
as soon as the seed is in
away from us he's going   [1846]
walk the way to Galway town
1810   find his passage on a ship
to send for us in a year
it is long his journey is
bábóg 6 months when he goes
Bridget is 11 years
1815   she will tend the younger ones
I will take Thady's work share
Ambrose' boy will cut the turf

working with John and Michael
we will not know where is he
1820 parted from his dear childer
it is that torments his heart
not ready is he to go
to leave the place where we are
not knowing will he see us
1825 sure, God be with the days so
he takes his bundle and goes
carrying his bit of food
walks to the west for 3 days
goes west to go farther west
1830 there was no way we could know
              May Day we garland the cow
chase the hag from the meadow
fresh wild greens to stir in meal
white flowers on the praties
1835 green blanket spotted with blooms
covering the lazy beds
the house garden well sprouted
neeps are nearly for digging
small round roots full of flavour
1840 can fill a belly with food
praties oats neeps and cabbage
the food we grow our own selves
berries cresses and sorrel
growing from God's own goodness
1845 milk butter eggs and bacon
what we get from the craythurs
all of it gives us our life
it gives us our bit of life
but the pratie is the thing

1850   the only thing to keep us
          on our small fields and leases
          only crop that grows enough
          keeps God between us and harm
          last year was a hard lost year
1855   next year Thady will have us
          this year we wait for July
                  And then the rain falls and falls
          keeps falling drenching the land
          hot weather and endless rain
1860   the turf cannot be drying
          the oats and hay are bowed down
          the warm dry ripening time
          gone hot and murderous wet
          the air so sticky it clings
1865   steams like kettles on the hob
          soaking drowning pratie beds
          the trenches full as rivers
          the praties sitting in mud
          the boys out up to their knees
1870   trying can they drain it off
          muise, 'tis a fret to us
          the old fear is upon us
          and then the heavy white fog
          comes crawling across the hills
1875   moving across the townlands
          passing over every field
          curling around every plant
          it is a fairy mischief
          is fairies in it surely
1880   a cloud spun of bean sí hair
          is shrouding every cottage

an evil class of a fog
the leaves show spots in 3 days
a coat of white fuzz beneath
1885   all trying can we stop it
the leaves and stalks turning black
hacking off the blighted plants
yanking praties from the ground
blessing with holy water
1890   God help us Mary help us
we hear the wailing coming
crying across the parish
the blight has come upon us
the crop rotting in our hands
1895   black as soot on a hearthside
fingers sinking in the slime
pigs and chickens won't eat them
the stench of rotten praties
sickens our hearts to the death
1900   only half a crop last year
and no crop at all this year
the oat field is thin and poor
a bitter harvest coming
           Yellow meal at market price
1905   driven higher every day
for sale at the shops in town
hucksters profit from hunger
walking 5 miles 30 miles
carry 2 stone of meal back
1910   a strange new food it is here
there's no taste for yellow meal
now they will eat anything
if they have ready money

sell their clothes their pots and tools
1915   paupers without a shilling
will get their death from hunger
it is famine is on us
landless women and childer
thin cipíns in their hunger
1920   grubbing in the rotted fields
searching for a few praties
to stop the childer crying
barely to keep life in them
offer a handful of spuds
1925   some meal for the love of God
my own stores are thin enough
neighbour can't let neighbour starve
is there a morsel of food
to spare from my childer's mouths
1930   talk churns along the bóithrín
the landlord it is will help
the government will save us
never something for nothing
talk never brought home the turf
1935   talk will never bring us food
where will the people get help
8d a day to labour
8d won't feed anyone
breaking stones and building walls
1940   around nothing roads nowhere
1 worker per family
gets a ticket for the works
if the committee chooses
at Samhain there are hundreds
1945   hundreds in Fiodharta parish

hungry and cold on the works
break rocks and dig holes all day
not a bite of food taken
it is a nation of slaves
1950 that is worked and starved to death
and their owners knowing it
spailpíns are starting to die
crawl into their huts and die
in corners by their childer
1955 hunger and famine sickness
hunger and sickness and cold
the sheep and pigs and cattle
sold half price herded to ports
snow falls deep as the river
1960 ice like a shell on the lake
cruel weather is on us
half dried turf makes a poor fire
we see the cloud of our breath
the cold biting at our feet
1965   Father Henry confesses   [1847]
crowds of souls along the road
Holy Mary with us now
agus ar uair ár mbáis[113]
the workhouse is a death house
1970 shelter alive with disease
full to bursting with paupers
landlords haven't paid their rates
the inmates go without food
please God help save the childer
1975 sure Thady must help us soon
the townlands under a shroud

---

[113][ah-gus err oor awr maw-ish]: and at the hour of our death

silent but for the groaning
the ground too frozen for graves
a plague of sickness coming
1980   priest anointing day and night
pleas on him my child my wife
someone is just departing
but the cold begins to break
Father Henry brings us news
1985   someone sent him the letter
because Thady cannot write
he is in New York City
he had work down by the ships
he cannot send us the fares
1990   Mother of God preserve us
         Thady's leg it is broken
there is a little money
he knows what is upon us
he prays we are all alive
1995   prays and cries a ghrá mo croidhe[114]
we have to stay still longer
he will send us what he can
to try can we pay the rent
we have a little oat seed
2000   praties for a little crop
hidden up in the rafters
guarding it like a treasure
the shame of hoarding my food
turning away the helpless
2005   never the way in the past
always a bite to offer
an egg or a bit of meal

---

[114][a graw ma cree]: love of my heart

never the way to refuse
the terrible choice it is
2010 the terrible choice is made
close the door to the hungry
the little bó will save us
the pig is sold to buy meal
I had no feed to spare it
2015 corn goes farther lasts longer
we look everywhere for food
when the ice is off the lake
Ambrose and Thady's good sons
trying would they catch a fish
2020 might be eel in the water
Ann needs hearty food to eat
neeps and cabbages long gone
my few small hens are eaten
stewed up for a little meat
2025 2 stolen by man or beast
soon new herbs will be growing
I can make a cure for Ann
ragwort and mallow and cress
mint would settle her belly
2030 she fades faster than spring comes
nettle tops would clean her blood
iris for famine fever
Celia keeps the other 4
keeps my childer safe away
2035 God between them and all harm
a sup of broth in her mouth
she is a rag in my arms
who was once a singing child

	broken in halves my heart is
2040	ochone mo mhuirnín mo croidhe
	this sorrow will stay with us
	our small daughter to have died
	we wake with her here ourselves
	no dúidíns and no crúiscin
2045	please God save her little soul
	wrap her in a scrap of cloth
	cover for her little bones
	pray the Rosary for her
	and then put her in the clay
2050	bury her from my bent back
	by Peter in the churchyard
	the churchyard like a plowed field
	so many just departing
	not a chance to have the priest
2055	our grief is still upon us
	the childer for their sister
	I for my laughing girleen
	trying to stay on the land
	trying not to find our death
2060	Put our few seeds in the ground
	a sorry bit of planting
	gather up every green thing
	chickweed cresses and clover
	the food of Fionn and Fergus[115]
2065	clean the blood and cure sickness
	the fields and meadows picked clean
	every riverbank stripped bare
	every leaf and every blade
	all over every townland

---

[115]a poet king; a figure in Irish myth

2070	into barely living mouths
	soon the bó will drop her calf
	don't know will we eat the calf
	will we sell it for some meal
	soon we'll have milk and butter
2075	little bó will save our lives
	we watch her every instant
	the paupers are on the road
	had to eat their bit of seed
	penniless seedless paupers
2080	missus buried her childer
	covered the bodies with rocks
	to save them from rats and dogs
	hundreds gone from the parish
	disappearing every day
2085	gone to the towns to beg food
	spit on the faith for a bowl
	converts for a bowl of soup
	perverted class of churchmen
	The devil is on the land
2090	lures the starving to be damned
	walking in their shreds of rags
	seeing and hearing nothing
	open-mouthed grógíns walking
	dying with grass in their mouths
2095	mad as Suibhne[116] with hunger
	sink themselves into the clay
	Father calls it all murder
	bliadhan an air[117] on the land
	it is a year of slaughter

---

[116][sweeny]: the mad king; a figure in Irish myth
[117][blee-uhn an ayr]: year of slaughter

2100	death rolling across the fields
	bean sí wails at every house
	tradesmen paid in food each year
	conacre to small farmer
	every house but the big house
2105	I saw with my mortal eyes
	desperate eating dead dogs
	starving dogs eating the dead
	fighting rats for the corpses
	lying unburied for days
2110	scavenger starlings and gulls
	all screeching over a share
	all of these horrors I saw
	like the púca had been loosed
	like God had forsaken us
2115	the barely alive hunting
	catching hedgehogs snaring hares
	set traps for birds and squirrels
	the little bog birds singing
	their songs from another time
2120	flitting to catch the insects
	John in the bog carting turf
	cut and footed a year since
	a few bricks against the cold
	a terrible season this
2125	8 years old a working man
	Celia's son is 20 years
	working on his mother's share
	Michael and John cut fresh spades
	little they have strength to do
2130	slow working in their hunger
	counting the days to July

Thady's bit of money comes
Ann is still living to him
he prays we are all alive
2135   pays the rent thanks be to God
starving people eat their rent
water should be thick with fish
golden rudd and red-finned perch
sweet and muddy bream and tench
2140   rich and firm and flaky meat
empty as our mouths it is
every fish netted and speared
we have one thing to feed us
the early crop is healthy
2145   the share of praties is sound
glory be thanks be to God
small planting makes small reaping
2 tons where we would have 8
it would need 8 to feed us
2150   our hope is in the oat field
strewn on 1st quality soil
the calf is sold to buy meal
those who had a grain to sow
and had not a £ for rent
2155   ejected after planting
decrees against the tenants
agents seizing the cattle
agents putting people out
tearing the roofs off houses
2160   people living in scalpeens[118]
driven to ground like badgers
pity them there half alive

---

[118] a hole in the ground with some sort of covering pulled over

a merciless ejectment
like a judge's death sentence
2165   better to be for the rope
death would be a friend to them
every third family here
is utterly destitute
half the parish owes the rent
2170   falls under the hanging gale[119]
some landlords shovelling out
cheaper to ship the tenants
over to the Kanadies
than to pay the Poor Law rates
2175   level townlands like forests
some few resident landlords
some kind people called Quakers
show God's mercy to the poor
                Vats of soup and yellow meal
2180   free to scrawny outstretched hands
not happening here along
over in Strokestown union
Major Mahon the landlord
a committee guardian
2185   clearing the estate he is
shovelling out those who will
ejecting those who will not
a vermin worse than Cromwell
happy to see them going
2190   killed by Molly Maguires he
killed for heartless clearing he
but if he was relief comes
the secret societies

---

[119]arrears in rent

```
              do revenge and robbery
     2195     the relief societies
              a gift from godly people
              never a government plan
              scheme to feed children in school
              the 5 schools in the parish
     2200     a ration of rice and meal
              to Bridget, John, and Martin
              fed from the school 3 seasons
              bit of clothes replace their rags
              there is mercy in the world
     2205     muise, God be with the days
              never have I lived a year
              never one that was blacker
              and if it was I pray God
              lift the curse is on the land
     2210     Thady there in the wide world              [1848]
              a far part of the wide world
              gone from us 2 years away
              it is a long time it is
              he is after striving there
     2215     we are after wasting here
              and our daughter died from us
              we scrabble here in the dirt
              he scrabbles there in the port
                        Father brings the new letter
     2220     we are here another year
              need money to pay the fares
              need money for food at sea
              captains give 1 pound a week
              1 pound of food a person
     2225     hungry here starving at sea
```

we plant our bit of praties
we spread our bit of oat seed
gather nettles and sorrel
the bounty of St. Caoimhín[120]
2230 and we keep ourselves alive
Thady keeps us paid in rent
offering for the sparán
blight again but not so fierce
we have a crop of praties
2235 better than the one before
the terror now not hunger
plague and fever ravaging
people in their weakness die
in silence receive their death
2240 the parish has gone silent
not a bird to fly or sing
not a voice to tell a tale
not a fish to leap and splash
not a hare or pig or calf
2245 spectres digging in silence
grinding the meal without sound
the breeze has no strength to blow
everything is spent it is
follow our faces the way
2250 do the bit of work the day
keep my 4 childer alive
until the last letter comes
            Enough now in the sparán   [1849]
we are for the road away
2255 my mother and my father
are perished of cholera

---

[120][kevin]: founder and first abbot of Glendalough

74

I have two brothers alive
Laurence home by the ring fort
up the hill from the churchyard
2260 living there by the ring fort
staying here in the parish
John is for emigrating
travelling into the west
Ambrose' boy is there planting
2265 between us we make the rent
Celia on her 2 acres
and her boy on ours beside
the bó will keep them alive
on the little An Linn Bhán
2270 the fire in our hearth still burns
God between them and all harm
wrap up our little bundles
our bits of rags and a pot
bits of food for the walking
2275 leave here with my dear childer
buy provisions in Galway
cheaper fare to Kanady
Thady won't know where are we
we will have to find him so
2280 who knows what ship will take us
what place it will take us to
after our weeks in steerage
God between us and all harm
we will get there all alive
2285 I am 35 years old
my name is Katie Murphy
Bridget a stór is 14
John is 10, Martin 7

Catherine is 3 years old
2290 Peter and Ann there behind
Peter and Ann in the clay
Thady across the water
five of us are sailing now
telling out our story now
2295 it is 1849

Glossary

a cushla geal mo chroidhe: [a cooshla gyall ma cree]: the vein, the pulse, the beating voice of my heart

a ghrá mo croidhe: [a graw ma cree]: love of my heart

a stór: [asthore]: treasure

ag iompar clainne: [aig umper klonyuh]: pregnant

agus ar uair ár mbáis: [ah-gus err oor awr maw-ish]: and at the hour of our death

Aibreán: [ab-rown]: April

airneán: [arneh-an]: gathering for talk

alt-luachra: [lew-kra]: an evil, greedy fairy

An Linn Bhán: [an linn bawn or vawn]: Linbaun River in Co. Roscommon

bábóg: [babogue]: baby

báibín: [babeen]: baby

báinín: [bawneen]: unbleached cloth

Ballinagare: [bal-in-a-gar]: a village in north-west Co. Roscommon

Bealtaine: [balltinna]: Summer

bean an tí: [banatee]: woman of the house

bean fionn: [ban finn]: a water fairy who will reach up and pull children under

bean sí: [banshee]: a fairy woman, death messenger

bheist: [beest]: waistcoat

brat Bhride: [brat breed]: Brigid's cloak

bliadhan an air: [blee-uhn an ayr]: year of slaughter

bó: [b-oh]: cow

bóithrín: [boreen]: country track

brachán neantóg: [brawkan nyantoke]: porridge of nettles and oatmeal

breith clainne: [b-zhay klonyuh]: childbirth

cáibín: [cawbeen]: hat

Caoilte: [kweeltuh]: a figure in Irish myth, a poet

cipíns: [chipeens]: kindling sticks

ciséan: [kihshawn]: tray-like basket for straining potatoes

clachan: [clah-hawn]: co-operative life among a cluster of cottages

clíabhs: [cleeves]: basket

Conall Cearnach: [cayr-nach]: chief warrior of the Red Branch, a
   figure in Irish myth

corn: any cereal grain

craythur: creature

creepies: three-legged stools

crúibin: [croobeen]: pig's foot

crúiscin: [croosh-keen]: a small jar or jug

d: pence

Daghda: [dagda]: a figure in Irish myth, whose cauldron is one of the
   four treasures

daoine sidhe: [deena shee]: people of the mounds, the Tuatha dé
   Dannan, the fairies

Deirdre: [derdruh]: defiant lover of Naoise; fated to sorrow; a figure
   in Irish myth

Diarmuid and Grainne: [deermud; grawnyuh]: wandering lovers;
   figures in Irish myth

dúidíns: [doodeens]: clay pipes

drisín: [drisheen]: a sort of black pudding, made from cow and sheep
   blood

drugget: coarse durable woolen cloth

Eanáir: [an-awr]: January

eddish: [ed-ish]: second-growth grass

éineacht: [aynukht]: done together

Feabhra: [favra]: February

Fiodharta: [fyurtee]: a parish in Co. Roscommon

Fionn and Fergus: [finn]; Fionn Mac Chumhaill of the Fianna and
   Fergus, the poet king; figures in Irish myth

forenent: over against
Fraochán: [frocken]: another name for bilberries
frieze: heavy woolen cloth

gaimbín: [gombeen]; wheeler dealer, usurer
Garland Sunday: the last Sunday of July
gawm: simpleton
go leór: [galore]: sufficiency
gogaire: [guggereh]: crouched, squatting
graip: [grape]: a shovel
Gráinne: [grawnyuh]: wandering lover, with Diarmuid; a figure in
    Irish myth
griscín: [griskeen]: pork loin
grógíns: [grogeens]: kindling sticks

hanging gale: arrears in rent
hearth crane: a bracket that can swivel pots over or away from the
    fire

Imbolc: [imbolk]: Spring

Kanadies: Upper and Lower Canada

laigh: [loy]: a hand plough with a foot rest and a curved blade
leanbh: [lannuv]: child
Lisnavalla: [lisnaville]: now called Lissaneaville
Lughnasa: [loonuhsa]: Autumn, harvest
lus an bhainne: [lus an vanyuh]: milkwort, a bluebell

meisce: [meshkyuh]: drunk
meitheal: [meh-hull]: communal labour
Mhaigh Eo: [mayoh]: Co. Mayo
mí na meala: [mee na meela]: month of honey
mo bhuachaill: [ma voo-a-kull]: my boy
mo croidhe: [ma-cree]: my heart

muise: [musha]: indeed

múinteoir: [monchoor]: teacher

neeps: turnips

Niamh: [neeuv]: daughter of Manannan Mac Lír, god of the sea; a
figure in Irish myth

Nollaig na mBan: [null-ag na man]: Women's Christmas

ochone: [och-ohn or o hone]: a sorrow from the past that is still
present

ochone mo mhuirnín mo croidhe: [o hone ma voorneen ma cree]:
oh sorrow, my darling, my heart

Oíche na Gaoíthe Móire: [eekhya na gweeha moyra]: The Night of
the Big Wind

Pádraig: [porig]: Patrick

pardógs: [par-dohgs]: large baskets

poc sí: [puck shee]: fairy struck

póitín: [potcheen]: traditional distilled drink

pot hake: a hook for hanging pots over the hearth

praties: potatoes

púca: [pooka]: feared and mischievous fairy

Ros Comáin: [ross-co-main]: Co. Roscommon

s: shillings

saining: protective birth rituals

Samhain: [sowuhn]: November, Winter

scalpeens: a hole in the ground with some sort of covering pulled
over

scraws: square sods

seamair óg: [shamrogue]: shamrock

sidhe: [shee]: people of the mounds, the Tuatha dé Dannan, the
fairies

sléan: [shlawn]: turf-cutting tool

slíbhín: [sleeveen]: an untrustworthy person
spailpín: [spalpeen]: a migratory labourer
sparán: [spa-rawn]: purse
sparógs: [spa-rohgs]: poor quality turf
St. Caoimhín: [kevin]:founder and first abbot of Glendalough
St. Cera: [kare-a or kee-ra]: an Irish abbess
St. Cíarán: St. Ciarán of Clonmacnoise, born in Fuerty, Co.
   Roscommon
stibhín: [steeveen]: a tool to make holes for potatoes
stone: 1 stone = 14 pounds
sugán: [shoo-gawn]: twisted straw
Suibhne: [sweeny]: a figure in Irish myth

Tae na gCailleach: [kye-luhkh]: wise hag, Celtic goddess of Winter
tar isteach: [tahr ish-tyahk]: come in
Thady: [tay-dy]: a familiar form for Timothy
tSuca: [sook]: a river in Co. Roscommon

weight: pounds

Acknowledgements

Deep gratitude to my Irish friends and advisors:
Albert Siggins, John Kelly, and Maureen Kenny in Fuerty Parish,
Roscommon; Dr. Ciarán Ó Murchadha in Galway and Clare

To my first reader:
Linda Tomlinson, who led me to believe I was making something

To my sister, my children, and my friends, who steadily encouraged
me.

For financial and practical support:
Canada Council for the Arts; Woodcock Fund (The Writers' Trust of
Canada); Banff Centre for the Arts

For access to print, microfilm, and objects:
Roscommon County Library; National Library of Ireland; National
Archive of Ireland; National Museum of Ireland (Country Life)

Historical Sources:
Griffith's Valuation (1847-1864); *Census of Elphin* (1749); *Shaw Mason's
Parochial Survey of Ireland* (1814); *Tithe Applotment Books* (1825);
Statistical Survey of the County of Roscommon (Isaac Weld 1832); *A
Topographical Dictionary of Ireland* (Samuel Lewis 1837); *Griffith's Field
Books* (1839); *The Destitution Survey* (1847)

Print Sources:
Ways of Old: Traditional Life in Ireland (Olive Sharkey 2000); *In Their*

Own Words: The Famine in North Connacht 1845-1849 (Liam Swords 1999); *Irish Wild Plants: Myths, Legends, & Folklore* (Niall Mac Coitir 2008); *Cuchulain Of Muirthemne* (Augusta Gregory 1902); *Gods and Fighting Men* (Augusta Gregory 1904); *Beside the Fire* (Douglas Hyde 1910); *The Night of the Big Wind* (Peter Carr 1933); *Irish Emigration 1801-1921* (David Fitzpatrick 1984); *Riotous Roscommon: Social Unrest in the 1840s* (Anne Colman 1999); *Roscommon Before the Famine* (William Gacquin 1996); *The Murder of Major Mahon, Strokestown, County Roscommon, 1847* (Padraig Vesey 2008); *Annals of the Famine in Ireland* (Asenath Nicholson 1998); *The Great Irish Famine* (Ed. Cathal Póirtéir 1995)

Photo: Linda Tomlinson

A. Mary Murphy's first book of poetry, *Shattered Fanatics,* was published in 2007. Her poetry has been published in numerous journals across Canada, the United States, France, Wales, and New Zealand including the *Antigonish Review, the Dalhousie Review, The Prairie Journal of Canadian Literature, Descant, Canadian Literature* and *Grain.* She teaches postsecondary classes in literature and film, leads travel study trips to Ireland, and has a freelance writing, editing, and mentoring business. She lives in Calgary, Alberta.